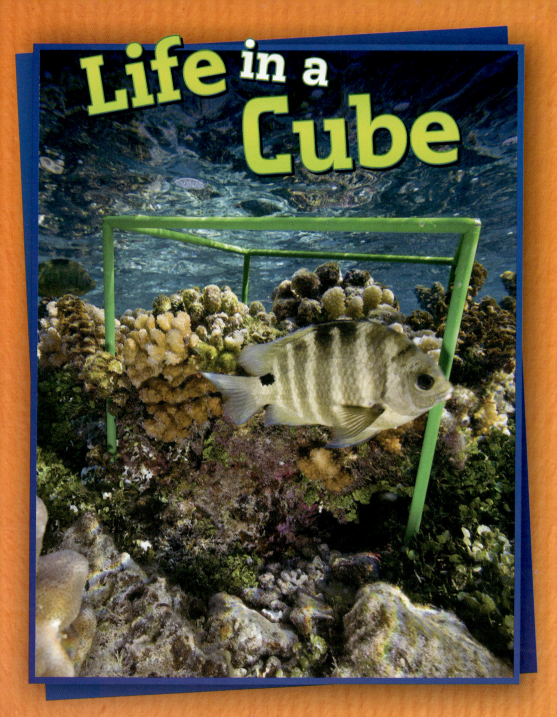

Life in a Cube

Seth Rogers

Contributing Author

Allison Duarte

Consultants

Christopher Meyer, Ph.D.
Research Zoologist
National Museum of Natural History

Stephanie Anastasopoulos, M.Ed.
TOSA, STREAM Integration
Solana Beach School District

Publishing Credits

Rachelle Cracchiolo, M.S.Ed., *Publisher*
Conni Medina, M.A.Ed., *Managing Editor*
Diana Kenney, M.A.Ed., NBCT, *Content Director*
Véronique Bos, *Creative Director*
Robin Erickson, *Art Director*
Michelle Jovin, M.A., *Associate Editor*
Mindy Duits, *Senior Graphic Designer*
Smithsonian Science Education Center

Image Credits: front cover, p.1, p.7 (top), p.9 (bottom), p.13 (bottom) David Liittschwager/National Geographic Creative; p.8 (top) Anand Varmar/National Geographic Creative; p.13 (top) Ted Kinsman/Science Source; p.15 (bottom) Visual&Written/Newscom; p.21 Oxford Scientific/Getty Images; p.25, p.32 (left) © Smithsonian; p.22 (bottom) Jessica Wilson/Science Source; p.23 (top) Alexis Rosenfeld/Science Source; p.23 (bottom) Burt Jones & Maurine Shimlock/Science Source; all other images from iStock and/or Shutterstock.

Library of Congress Cataloging-in-Publication Data

Names: Rogers, Seth, author.
Title: Life in a cube / Seth Rogers.
Description: Huntington Beach, CA : Teacher Created Materials, Inc., [2019] | Audience: Grade 4 to 6. | Includes index. |
Identifiers: LCCN 2018018113 (print) | LCCN 2018020183 (ebook) | ISBN 9781493869473 (E-book) | ISBN 9781493867073 (paperback)
Subjects: LCSH: Habitat (Ecology)--Observations--Juvenile literature.
Classification: LCC QH541.14 (ebook) | LCC QH541.14 .R64 2019 (print) | DDC 577--dc23
LC record available at https://lccn.loc.gov/2018018113

© 2019 Smithsonian Institution. The name "Smithsonian" and the Smithsonian logo are registered trademarks owned by the Smithsonian Institution.

Teacher Created Materials

5301 Oceanus Drive
Huntington Beach, CA 92649-1030
www.tcmpub.com

ISBN 978-1-4938-6707-3

© 2019 Teacher Created Materials, Inc.
Printed in China
Nordica.102018.CA21801129

Table of Contents

More than Meets the Eye 4

Thinking inside the Box 9

Trip to a Coral Reef 14

Trouble in Paradise 21

One Step at a Time 27

STEAM Challenge 28

Glossary 30

Index 31

Career Advice 32

Central Park

More than Meets the Eye

Everybody knows there is life on Earth…a *lot* of life. In fact, no one knows exactly how many different living things are on Earth. Even today, people are still finding new species. Life is all around us, no matter where we are. From the largest life forms to the tiniest creatures, studying all living things can seem impossible.

red-tailed hawk

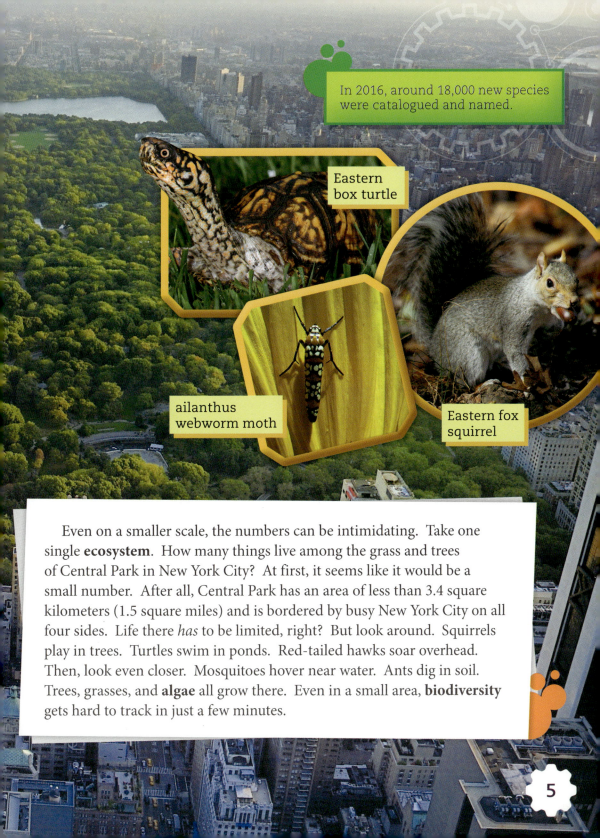

In 2016, around 18,000 new species were catalogued and named.

Eastern box turtle

ailanthus webworm moth

Eastern fox squirrel

Even on a smaller scale, the numbers can be intimidating. Take one single **ecosystem**. How many things live among the grass and trees of Central Park in New York City? At first, it seems like it would be a small number. After all, Central Park has an area of less than 3.4 square kilometers (1.5 square miles) and is bordered by busy New York City on all four sides. Life there *has* to be limited, right? But look around. Squirrels play in trees. Turtles swim in ponds. Red-tailed hawks soar overhead. Then, look even closer. Mosquitoes hover near water. Ants dig in soil. Trees, grasses, and **algae** all grow there. Even in a small area, **biodiversity** gets hard to track in just a few minutes.

You may be asking yourself, *How can people possibly study all life in an ecosystem when there is so much of it?* Photographer David Liittschwager had the same question so he came up with a new idea. Rather than trying to record data about life in an ecosystem, he decided to start small. He wanted to work with a sample size that could fit in his lap. He decided to build a cube with a volume of about 28 liters (1 cubic foot). He explored this idea in his book *A World in One Cubic Foot*.

The idea is simple. The smaller a sample size is, the closer it can be observed. More time can be spent looking at life that usually hides from view. But Liittschwager needed each sample to be an equal size so he could compare his results. He had to make many decisions. First, he asked which living things should be counted and which should not? Next, he had to choose places to study. Liittschwager wanted to find areas where there was as much biodiversity as possible. That would give him more life to study in each ecosystem.

wood duck

black-throated green warbler

Liittschwager's cube in Central Park

rat

Eastern tiger swallowtail

SCIENCE

A Delicate Balance

Small parts of an ecosystem can be filled with life. But they cannot stand on their own. Each part depends on other living and nonliving things around it. This **interdependence** is why it is so important to keep balance within an ecosystem. One small change in one part of an ecosystem can have widespread and long-lasting effects on the rest.

Liittschwager examines a fish in Moorea, French Polynesia.

Thinking inside the Box

Liittschwager next set the process for his project. First, he would place his cube-shaped frame in a **habitat** where it could be observed. Liittschwager would set his cube in places that were wild and overgrown. He knew these places would have the most biodiversity. He would leave the cube in each location for 24 hours. Every living thing that passed through the cube would be recorded. Samples of each life form would be collected and photographed. These samples would then be returned to where they were found. He'd follow this same process in each location. That way, he could compare his results.

Liittschwager wanted each location in his book to be **unique**. He wanted to show life in a wide range of places. He thought this would make readers wonder what might be hiding in their own backyards. He asked **biologists** and **botanists** to help him pick the best places for his project. They helped him choose five types of habitats. Those habitats would give Liittschwager the best samples for his book. And one of these habitats changed how Liittschwager saw the world.

TECHNOLOGY
Simple, Yet Effective

At the center of Liittschwager's project was his cube. The cube had to be visible, but it had to blend into the natural landscape of many locations too. It also had to be sturdy enough to withstand the outdoor conditions of the project. In the end, he made the cube with 12 stainless steel rods. The rods could be put together and taken apart as needed. Then, the cube was painted green to help it blend in with its surroundings.

The first habitat Liittschwager visited was in the leaf litter of a forest. Leaf litter consists of leaves, twigs, and pieces of bark that have fallen to the ground. Most people walk over leaves and never think about what is underneath. But huge amounts of life can be found in leaf litters. Liittschwager chose a section of Central Park to record his data. He placed his cube and waited. Squirrels, slugs, insects, and birds came to the cube while he watched. Overnight, the cube had even been picked up and moved by a raccoon!

raccoon

Central Park, United States

Another habitat Liittschwager observed was **shrubland**. He went to Table Mountain in the Cape Floral region of South Africa for this photo shoot. The land there is much drier than it is in Central Park. But Cape Floral is still full of **diverse** life. Three percent of all the plants in Africa can be found there. These plants attract a wide range of insects and spiders. Liittschwager knew he would come across a completely different ecosystem there than he had in New York City.

Black girdled lizards can only be found at Table Mountain.

king protea blossom

Some plants that grow in shrubland have **adapted** to survive the forest fires that are common there.

Table Mountain, South Africa

Liittschwager also visited a cloud forest **canopy**. He traveled to Costa Rica to place his cube high up on the branch of a tree. Below his cube lay the dark and shady forest floor. But the canopy was different. It was much warmer and drier. There was much more sunlight in the canopy than there was on the forest floor below. Life in the canopy looked very different than it did on the forest floor. Beetles and moths flew from leaf to leaf. Centipedes and ghost spiders crawled along the branches of the trees.

ARTS

Nowhere to Hide

One thing that stands out as you flip through *A World in One Cubic Foot* is the images. The plants and animals are shown on plain white backgrounds. This detail came from Liittschwager's love of scientific illustrations. These drawings are completed on a plain white background so the details of the samples are easier to see. Liittschwager wanted his photographs to have the same effect.

centipede

Liittschwager also visited two **aquatic** habitats. One was a freshwater river. Freshwater rivers are filled with life. That is especially true for Duck River in Tennessee. Duck River is home to several species that cannot be found anywhere else on Earth. That is because Duck River has been flowing for millions of years. Many living things in the river might be missed at first glance. But Liittschwager's cube found shelled mussels, clams, and snails that looked like rocks. He also found water pennies. These beetle larvae looked more like fossils than living things.

water penny beetle larva

While at Duck River, Liittschwager's cube recorded this fish.

Trip to a Coral Reef

The second aquatic habitat Liittschwager took his cube to was a coral reef off the island of Moorea in French Polynesia. This is one of the most important habitats on Earth. It was on Moorea that he met **zoologist** Chris Meyer. He works for the Smithsonian Institution. Meyer helped Liittschwager identify samples in the cube.

Meyer was also the **coordinator** of the Biocode Project. The aim of this project was to identify all species on and around Moorea. Meyer did this by collecting **DNA** samples. Liittschwager's cube helped Meyer as well. All the life that passed through the cube was recorded for the Biocode Project.

In all, they found more than six hundred species in one cubic foot of coral reef. This was just a small amount of the life that lives in the reef. Thousands of plankton swam through the cube. But they were less than a millimeter (four-hundredths of an inch) in size. These tiny creatures were impossible to collect. It was also hard to choose a place to set the cube. If it had been placed just one or two meters over, life in the cube would have been very different.

Squat lobsters are common in Moorea.

Different species of fish swim through coral in Moorea.

Lemonpeel angelfish live in and around the coral in Moorea.

Moorea is just 1 of the 118 islands that make up French Polynesia.

Liittschwager learned a lot from his trip to the coral reef. Reefs are one of the most diverse habitats in the world. Coral reefs only exist in a narrow band around the equator. This part of the ocean is very low in **nutrients**. Because of this, it is sometimes called a "liquid desert." In other areas of the ocean, water is a cloudy green color. This is due to the **phytoplankton** (figh-toh-PLANK-tuhn) that grows in the water. But since there are so few nutrients in water near the equator, phytoplankton cannot live. This makes water in this part of the ocean a bright, clear blue.

coral polyps on frogspawn coral

tentacles on coral polyps

frogspawn coral

Despite its lack of nutrients, coral reefs are packed with life. Scientists think more than one million species live in or around coral reefs. Coral reefs are made up of coral polyps. A coral polyp is a tiny creature, no bigger than a bean. It lives on the ocean floor. Many coral polyps connect to one another and form a thin layer. Then, they produce calcium structures that build up over time. These structures help form coral reefs. Many larger animals depend on these structures for homes.

coral reef with different types of coral

MATHEMATICS

Pacing Polyps

Different types of coral polyps grow at different speeds. The fastest growing coral is staghorn coral. It builds structures that look like antlers. They can grow about 20 centimeters (8 inches) per year. Massive coral are the slowest growing species. Their structures look like giant boulders. Massive coral grow about 10 times slower than staghorn coral—about 5 to 25 mm (0.2–1 in.) per year.

Parts of a Coral Polyp

- tentacles for capturing prey
- stinging cells for capturing prey
- jelly-like substance for maintaining form
- mouth for releasing waste
- nutrient-producing algae
- layer of cells for absorbing nutrients and releasing waste
- gel for protection and capturing prey
- tissue that lets polyps share nutrients

Coral polyps build coral reefs and are related to jellyfish and sea anemones.

Many animals need coral reef structures to survive. Once coral polyps have formed a coral reef's skeleton, other forms of life can begin to thrive. Sea grasses from the sea floor grow around coral. They offer food and shelter to many more animals.

There are two types of algae that grow in coral reefs as well: single-celled and multi-celled algae. Single-celled algae live inside coral polyps. They help build coral structures. These algae use the sun to make sugars, which boost the energy of polyps. Multi-celled algae grow on the surface of coral. They help make the reef strong. Both types give coral reefs the bright colors they are known for.

Almost a fourth of all ocean life is thought to live in or near coral reefs. Fish, sea turtles, dolphins, and manatees all spend time living in or finding food there. Every living thing in a coral reef contributes to the health of the habitat. But recently, the balance of life in many coral reefs has been thrown off.

A snorkeler swims alongside a manatee.

White coral has lost its algae.

Brown coral is dead.

Scientists believe that three-fourths of the world's coral reefs are threatened. By 2030, nine-tenths could be threatened.

Trouble in Paradise

Luckily, the coral reef Liittschwager studied is still relatively healthy. But that is not true of all coral. Changes in the ocean's temperature and carbon dioxide levels are throwing coral reefs out of balance. Scientists are working hard to learn what is happening to coral reefs and how people can keep them safe.

Three major events in the past 20 years have affected coral reefs. These are called coral bleaching events. Coral bleaching is when normally bright and colorful reefs begin to turn white. This happens when water around reefs gets too warm. Polyps react to this change by ejecting the algae that live inside the reefs. Loss of algae is what makes coral turn white. But loss of color is not the biggest change taking place. Polyps can't get enough food on their own. They depend on nutrients from algae. Without algae, polyps begin to starve and die.

Once coral polyps die, reefs turn brown. New algae grow on the outside of the coral. However, instead of helping the coral thrive, these algae destroy them. As coral get destroyed, larger animals that depend on them leave or die as well.

Algae on coral polyps create oxygen and other nutrients for the coral.

Since 1998, there have been three global coral bleaching events. These events have happened closer together each time. As ocean temperatures rise, scientists fear that bleaching events will soon happen each year. Coral bleaching combined with over-fishing and water **pollution** could affect the entire planet.

The loss of coral would affect people. In many places, people depend on fish as their main food source. But if coral reefs start to die, fish will leave. This will cause some people to go hungry.

Dying coral reefs would also cause a loss of medicine. Scientists use parts of coral reefs to make medications. These medicines can treat cancers and other illnesses. More people will suffer without reefs.

The loss of coral would also affect land. Some coastal areas could be in danger. Oceans can have powerful **currents**. Reefs slow these currents and calm waters on shores. Without reefs to slow water, shores would be changed forever.

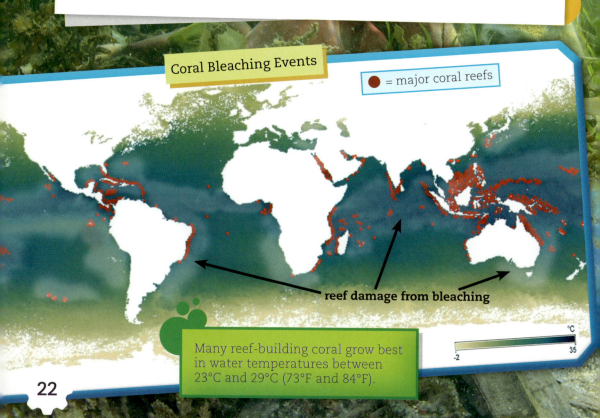

Coral Bleaching Events

● = major coral reefs

reef damage from bleaching

Many reef-building coral grow best in water temperatures between 23°C and 29°C (73°F and 84°F).

Biochemist Sophie Richter studies coral bleaching and its causes.

This brain coral is partway through a bleaching event.

Scientists are calling on people to help save coral reefs. Projects like Liittschwager's bring attention to the problem. But it is up to people to change their ways. If they don't, scientists think almost all of the world's coral reefs will die by the year 2050.

Luckily, there are groups working to help save reefs. They offer ways for everyone to help. First, people can build adaptive reefscapes. The goal of this project is to create healthy landscapes of coral reefs by putting different types of coral in the same reef. Some coral polyps are better than others at adapting to pollution. Others can survive longer in warmer water. Still, others can withstand larger waves. Adaptive reefscapes put these different types of coral together. Reefs will be able to adapt to any danger they face.

In other places, scientists are trying coral transplants. With this system, scientists take healthy coral polyps and grow them in tanks. Then, they wait until the polyps are old enough to **reproduce** on their own. Scientists carefully place the polyps back with bleached coral in the sea. The healthy coral are able to re-attach to the reef and bring the reef back to life.

Parrotfish clean coral by eating algae and dead coral.

A brittle star protects a coral reef.

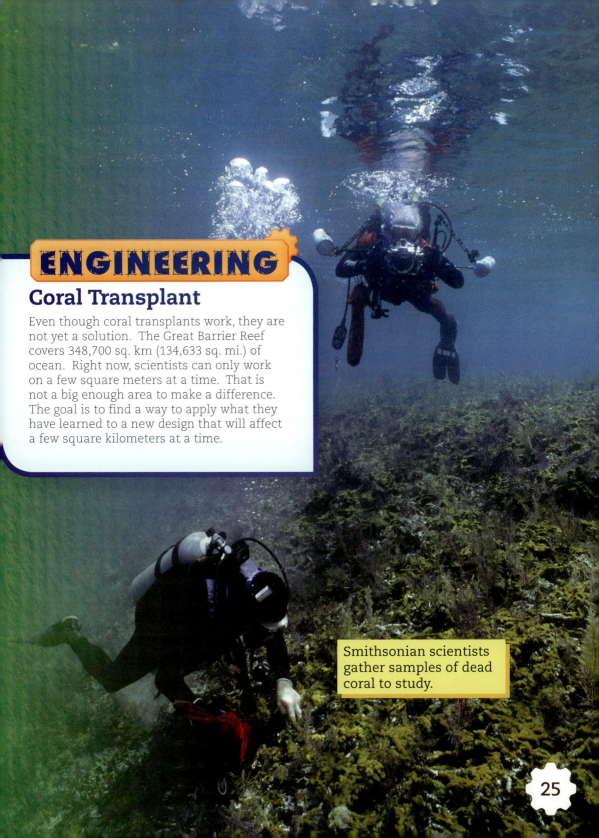

ENGINEERING
Coral Transplant
Even though coral transplants work, they are not yet a solution. The Great Barrier Reef covers 348,700 sq. km (134,633 sq. mi.) of ocean. Right now, scientists can only work on a few square meters at a time. That is not a big enough area to make a difference. The goal is to find a way to apply what they have learned to a new design that will affect a few square kilometers at a time.

Smithsonian scientists gather samples of dead coral to study.

The average depth of the San Francisco Bay is only about 6 m (17 ft.). However, the deepest part of the Bay is about 92 m (300 ft.).

One Step at a Time

Seeing the coral reef changed Liittschwager's project. He was not done yet. Three years after his trip, he decided to add a sixth location to his book. He had taken pictures at some of the most **exotic** places on Earth. This time, he wanted to test his project closer to home. He wanted to see what he would find in his home city of San Francisco, California. He took his cube and placed it in the bay near the Golden Gate Bridge. He found an ecosystem that was bursting with life. Every drop of water was full of tiny plankton. He found about nine thousand life forms living in one cubic foot of water in the bay.

Liittschwager's project has grown beyond his book. Students and scientists have re-created his project in their own neighborhoods. People are finding life they never noticed before in their local parks and streams. Even places they thought they knew inside and out had life hiding just beyond view. What is hiding just beyond your view? Find out more about your habitat. All you need to start is a cube.

STEAM CHALLENGE

Define the Problem

Life can be found all around us. It is easier to see creatures that would normally hide from view when your sample size is small. Your task is to create a 30 cm × 30 cm × 30 cm (1 ft. × 1 ft. × 1 ft.) cubic frame and re-create Liittschwager's experiment in your local area.

Constraints: Your cube's length, width, and height must measure exactly 30 cm (or exactly 1 ft.) each.

Criteria: Your cube must be durable and waterproof to withstand possible weather conditions. It should blend with its surroundings and be placed where it will have the most biodiversity pass through it.

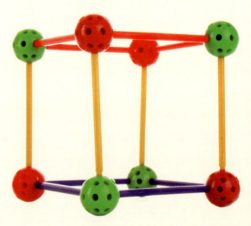

1. Research and Brainstorm

What materials would work best to build your cube? How will you construct it? Where will you place your cube? How will you photograph the samples you find? How will you replace samples when you are finished?

2. Design and Build

Choose where to place your cube. Where would the most biodiversity likely be? What color will you paint your cube to make it blend in with its environment? Build your cube.

3. Test and Improve

Test your cube's durability by spraying it with water and dropping it from 1 meter (1 yard) high. Did your cube stay dry and in one piece? If not, modify your design. Place your cube outdoors, and observe it for at least two hours over the course of one week. Take pictures or make detailed observations to keep a record. Was your cube placed in a good location? Was it difficult to observe your samples?

4. Reflect and Share

Create a museum exhibit that displays your cube and the photos and observations from your project. Include a short summary that explains where you placed your cube and what you found. What might have happened if you had chosen a different location? What if you left your cube outside for longer?

Glossary

adapted—changed to be able to live in a certain place or situation better

algae—simple plants or plantlike organisms that have no stems or leaves and that grow in or near water

aquatic—relating to plants and animals that live in or near water

biodiversity—the presence of many different types of plants and animals in an environment

biologists—scientists who study things that are alive

botanists—scientists who study plants

canopy—the highest layer of branches on trees or in a forest

coordinator—a person who organizes things or people

currents—continuous movements of water in the same direction

diverse—varied

DNA—a substance that carries genetic information in the cells of humans, animals, and plants

ecosystem—a community of living and nonliving things in a particular environment

ejecting—forcing out

exotic—from another part of the world

habitat—the area where a plant or an animal lives

interdependence—the state of needing or depending on one another

nutrients—substances that help people, animals, or plants grow

phytoplankton—microscopic marine algae

pollution—the process of making water, land, or air dirty and unsafe to use

reproduce—to make babies, new plants, or young animals

shrubland—a habitat where shrubs and bushes are the main vegetation

thrive—to develop or grow successfully

unique—very unusual or special

zoologist—a person who studies animals and animal behavior

Index

adaptive reefscapes, 24

algae, 5, 18, 20–21, 24

A World in One Cubic Foot, 6, 12

Biocode Project, 14

Central Park, 4–5, 7, 10–11

coral reef, 14, 16–18, 20–22, 24–25, 27

coral transplants, 24–25

Costa Rica, 12

Duck River, 13

French Polynesia, 8, 14–15

Golden Gate Bridge, 27

Great Barrier Reef, 25

leaf litter, 10

Liittschwager, David, 6–14, 16, 21, 24, 27

Meyer, Chris, 14

Moorea, 8, 14–15

New York City, 5, 11

phytoplankton, 16

San Francisco Bay, 26

shrubland, 11

Smithsonian, 14, 25

South Africa, 11

Table Mountain, 11

Tennessee, 13

CAREER ADVICE
from Smithsonian

Do you want to study life-forms?
Here are some tips to get you started.

"When I was a kid, I had shoeboxes full of baseball cards, sand from beaches, and anything else I could find. Today, my job is still to collect and study things, such as marine life in Moorea. I see my job like a huge scavenger hunt. Start collecting and studying objects now. You will find it is very rewarding to pursue questions you are curious about." —*Chris Meyer, Research Zoologist*

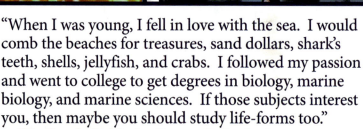

"When I was young, I fell in love with the sea. I would comb the beaches for treasures, sand dollars, shark's teeth, shells, jellyfish, and crabs. I followed my passion and went to college to get degrees in biology, marine biology, and marine sciences. If those subjects interest you, then maybe you should study life-forms too."
—*Dr. Carole Baldwin, Research Zoologist*